Jane Austen

Michael O'Mara Books Limited

But lovely as I was, the Graces of my Person were the
least of my Perfections. Of every accomplishment
accustomary to my sex, I was Mistress.

LOVE AND FREINDSHIP [SIC], 1790

'It tells me nothing that does not either vex or weary me.
The quarrels of popes and kings, with wars or pestilences,
in every page; the men all so good for nothing, and hardly any
women at all – it is very tiresome; and yet I often think it odd
that it should be so dull, for a great deal of it must be invention.
The speeches that are put into the heroes' mouths, their thoughts
and designs – the chief of all this must be invention.'

CATHERINE MORLAND, *NORTHANGER ABBEY*, 1818

'It is very difficult for the prosperous to be humble.'

FRANK CHURCHILL, *EMMA*, 1816

'One cannot have too large a party. A large party secures its own amusement.'

EMMA, EMMA, 1816

Husbands and wives generally understand when opposition will be vain.

PERSUASION, 1818

'If things are going untowardly one month, they are sure to mend the next.'

MR WESTON, *EMMA*, 1816

A good man must feel, how wretched, and how unpardonable, how hopeless, and how wicked it was to marry without affection.

MANSFIELD PARK, 1814

I mean to go to as many balls as possible, that I may have a good bargain.

LETTER TO CASSANDRA, 9 DECEMBER 1808

'What wild imaginations one forms where dear self
is concerned! How sure to be mistaken!'

ANNE ELLIOT, *PERSUASION*, 1818

She was nothing more than a mere good-tempered, civil
and obliging young woman; as such we could scarcely
dislike her – she was only an Object of Contempt.

LOVE AND FREINDSHIP [SIC], 1790

Woman is fine for her own satisfaction alone. No man will admire her the more, no woman will like her the better for it. Neatness and fashion are enough for the former, and a something of shabbiness or impropriety will be most endearing to the latter.

NORTHANGER ABBEY, 1818

'I cannot speak well enough to be unintelligible.'

CATHERINE MORLAND, *NORTHANGER ABBEY*, 1818

'Poverty is a great evil; but to a woman of education and feeling it ought not, it cannot be the greatest. I would rather be a teacher at a school (and I can think of nothing worse) than marry a man I did not like.'

EMMA, *THE WATSONS*, 1871

Dress is at all times a frivolous distinction, and excessive
solicitude about it often destroys its own aim.

NORTHANGER ABBEY, 1818

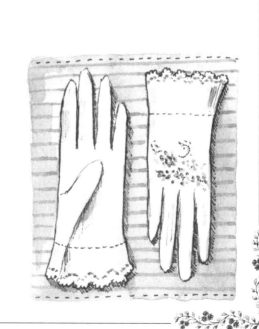

'One man's ways may be as good as another's, but we all like our own best.'

ADMIRAL CROFT, *PERSUASION*, 1818

Because they were fond of reading, she fancied them satirical: perhaps without exactly knowing what it was to be satirical; but THAT did not signify.

SENSE AND SENSIBILITY, 1811

Walter Scott has no business to write novels, especially good ones. It is not fair. He has fame and profit enough as a poet, and should not be taking the bread out of other people's mouths.

LETTER TO ANNA AUSTEN, 28 SEPTEMBER 1814

'They are much to be pitied who have not been taught to feel,
in some degree, as you do; who have not, at least, been given
a taste for Nature in early life. They lose a great deal.'

EDMUND BERTRAM, *MANSFIELD PARK*, 1814

I have just received nearly twenty pounds myself on the second edition
of *Sense and Sensibility* which gives me fine flow of literary ardour.

LETTER TO CAROLINE AUSTEN, 14 MARCH 1817

Seldom, very seldom, does complete truth belong to any human disclosure; seldom can it happen that something is not a little disguised, or a little mistaken.

EMMA, 1816

Let other pens dwell on guilt and misery. I quit such odious subjects as soon as I can, impatient to restore everybody, not greatly in fault themselves, to tolerable comfort, and to have done with all the rest.

MANSFIELD PARK, 1814

Man only can be aware of the insensibility of man towards a new gown.

NORTHANGER ABBEY, 1818

A mind lively and at ease, can do with seeing nothing,
and can see nothing that does not answer.

EMMA, 1816

It would be an excellent match, for HE was rich, and SHE was handsome.

SENSE AND SENSIBILITY, 1811

Provided that nothing like useful knowledge could be gained
from them, provided they were all story and no reflection,
she had never any objection to books at all.

NORTHANGER ABBEY, 1818, OF CATHERINE MORLAND

'What is right to be done cannot be done too soon.'

MR WESTON, *EMMA*, 1816

'Pray, my dear aunt, what is the difference in matrimonial
affairs, between the mercenary and the prudent motive?
Where does discretion end, and avarice begin?'

ELIZABETH BENNET, *PRIDE AND PREJUDICE*, 1813

'Money can only give happiness where there is nothing else to give it.'

MARIANNE DASHWOOD, *SENSE AND SENSIBILITY*, 1811

From the time of their sitting down to table, it was
a quick succession of busy nothings.

MANSFIELD PARK, 1814

My hair was at least tidy, which was all my ambition.

LETTER TO CASSANDRA, 20-1 NOVEMBER 1800

'But your mind is warped by an innate principle of general integrity, and therefore not accessible to the cool reasonings of family partiality, or a desire of revenge.'

HENRY TILNEY, *NORTHANGER ABBEY*, 1818

Matrimony, as the origin of change, was always disagreeable.

EMMA, 1816

'I had not known you a month before I felt that you were the last man in the world whom I could ever be prevailed on to marry.'

ELIZABETH BENNET, *PRIDE AND PREJUDICE*, 1813

'Happiness in marriage is entirely a matter of chance.'

CHARLOTTE LUCAS, *PRIDE AND PREJUDICE*, 1813

Nothing can be compared to the misery of being bound
without love – bound to one – and preferring another.

LETTER TO FANNY KNIGHT, 30 NOVEMBER 1814

'One cannot always be laughing at a man without now
and then stumbling on something witty.'

ELIZABETH BENNET, *PRIDE AND PREJUDICE*, 1813

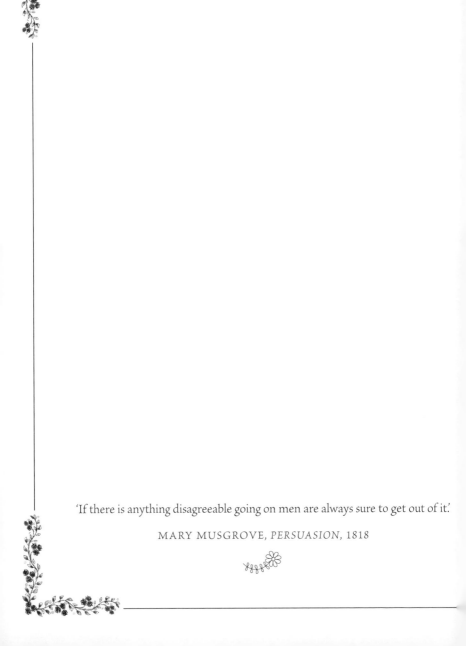

'If there is anything disagreeable going on men are always sure to get out of it.'

MARY MUSGROVE, *PERSUASION*, 1818

'Queen Elizabeth,' said Mrs Stanley, who never hazarded
a remark on history that was not well founded, 'lived
to a good old age, and was a very clever woman.'

CATHARINE, 1792

'I never heard a young lady spoken of for the first time, without being informed that she was very accomplished.'

MR BINGLEY, *PRIDE AND PREJUDICE*, 1813

'We certainly do not forget you as soon as you forget us.'

ANNE ELLIOT, *PERSUASION*, 1818

'The person, be it gentleman or lady, who has not pleasure
in a good novel, must be intolerably stupid.'

CATHERINE MORLAND, *NORTHANGER ABBEY*, 1818

It is a truth universally acknowledged, that a single man in possession of a good fortune, must be in want of a wife.

PRIDE AND PREJUDICE, 1813

'If I loved you less, I might be able to talk about it more.'

MR KNIGHTLEY, *EMMA*, 1816

I bought some Japan ink likewise, and next week shall begin my operations on my hat, on which you know my principal hopes of happiness depend.

LETTER TO CASSANDRA, 27-8 OCTOBER 1798

'For what do we live, but to make sport for our neighbours, and laugh at them in our turn?'

MR BENNET, *PRIDE AND PREJUDICE*, 1813

'To sit in the shade on a fine day, and look upon verdure, is the most perfect refreshment.'

FANNY PRICE, *MANSFIELD PARK*, 1814

'There is nothing I would not do for those who are really my friends.
I have no notion of loving people by halves, it is not my nature.'

ISABELLA THORPE, *NORTHANGER ABBEY*, 1818

I do not want people to be very agreeable, as it saves
me the trouble of liking them a great deal.

LETTER TO CASSANDRA, 24-6 DECEMBER 1798

'Nothing is more deceitful,' said Darcy, 'than the appearance of humility. It is often only carelessness of opinion, and sometimes an indirect boast.'

MR DARCY, *PRIDE AND PREJUDICE*, 1813

'Vanity working on a weak head, produces every sort of mischief.'

MR KNIGHTLEY, *EMMA*, 1816

'A lady's imagination is very rapid; it jumps from admiration to love, from love to matrimony in a moment.'

MR DARCY, *PRIDE AND PREJUDICE*, 1813

'Selfishness must always be forgiven, you know,
because there is no hope of a cure.'

MARY CRAWFORD, *MANSFIELD PARK*, 1814

'People who suffer as I do from nervous complaints can have no
great inclination for talking. Nobody can tell what I suffer! But it
is always so. Those who do not complain are never pitied.'

MRS BENNET, *PRIDE AND PREJUDICE*, 1813

'In vain have I struggled. It will not do. My feelings will not be repressed. You must allow me to tell you how ardently I admire and love you.'

MR DARCY, *PRIDE AND PREJUDICE*, 1813

'The more I know of the world, the more I am convinced that I shall never see a man whom I can really love. I require so much!'

MARIANNE DASHWOOD, *SENSE AND SENSIBILITY*, 1811

'We do not look in great cities for our best morality.'

EDMUND BERTRAM, *MANSFIELD PARK*, 1814

'If people like to read their books, it is all very well, but to be at so much trouble in filling great volumes, which, as I used to think, nobody would willingly ever look into, to be labouring only for the torment of little boys and girls, always struck me as a hard fate.'

CATHERINE MORLAND, *NORTHANGER ABBEY*, 1818

Here I am once more in this scene of dissipation and vice,
and I begin already to find my morals corrupted.

LETTER TO CASSANDRA ON ARRIVING
IN LONDON, 23 AUGUST 1796

'Nobody, who has not been in the interior of a family, can say what the difficulties of any individual of that family may be.'

EMMA, *EMMA*, 1816

'Vanity and pride are different things, though the words
are often used synonymously. A person may be proud without
being vain. Pride relates more to our opinion of ourselves;
vanity to what we would have others think of us.'

MARY BENNET *PRIDE AND PREJUDICE, 1813*

'You could not have made the offer of your hand in any possible way that would have tempted me to accept it.'

ELIZABETH BENNET, *PRIDE AND PREJUDICE*, 1813

A lady, without a family, was the very best preserver of furniture in the world.

PERSUASION, 1818

'What are men to rocks and mountains?'

ELIZABETH BENNET, *PRIDE AND PREJUDICE*, 1813

'Mr. Wickham is blessed with such happy manners as may ensure his making friends – whether he may be equally capable of retaining them, is less certain.'

MR DARCY, *PRIDE AND PREJUDICE*, 1813

'Why not seize the pleasure at once? How often is happiness
destroyed by preparation, foolish preparation!'

FRANK CHURCHILL, *EMMA*, 1816

'Silly things do cease to be silly if they are done by
sensible people in an impudent way.'

EMMA, *EMMA*, 1816

'I always deserve the best treatment because I never put up with any other.'

EMMA, *EMMA*, 1816

'One half of the world cannot understand the pleasures of the other.'

EMMA, *EMMA*, 1816

'A person who can write a long letter with ease, cannot write ill.'

MISS BINGLEY, *PRIDE AND PREJUDICE*, 1813

'It is particularly incumbent on those who never change their opinion, to be secure of judging properly at first.'

ELIZABETH BENNET, *PRIDE AND PREJUDICE*, 1813

'Stupid men are the only ones worth knowing after all.'

ELIZABETH BENNET, *PRIDE AND PREJUDICE*, 1813

Which of all my important nothings shall I tell you first?

LETTER TO CASSANDRA, 15 JUNE 1808

'Think only of the past as its remembrance gives you pleasure.'

ELIZABETH BENNET, *PRIDE AND PREJUDICE*, 1813

'I wish, as well as everybody else, to be perfectly happy; but, like everybody else, it must be in my own way.'

ELINOR DASHWOOD, *SENSE AND SENSIBILITY*, 1811

The real evils, indeed, of Emma's situation were the power of having rather too much her own way, and a disposition to think a little too well of herself.

EMMA, 1816

How quick come the reasons for approving what we like!

PERSUASION, 1818

'A man does not recover from such a devotion of the heart
to such a woman! He ought not; he does not.'

CAPTAIN WENTWORTH, *PERSUASION*, 1818

'Without music, life would be a blank to me.'

MRS ELTON, *EMMA*, 1816

'Surprizes are foolish things. The pleasure is not enhanced,
and the inconvenience is often considerable.'

MR KNIGHTLEY, *EMMA*, 1816

'A man who has nothing to do with his own time has no conscience in his intrusion on that of others.'

MARIANNE DASHWOOD, *SENSE AND SENSIBILITY*, 1811

'That would be the greatest misfortune of all! To find a
man agreeable whom one is determined to hate!'

ELIZABETH BENNET, *PRIDE AND PREJUDICE*, 1813

'Follies and nonsense, whims and inconsistencies do divert
me, I own, and I laugh at them whenever I can.'

ELIZABETH BENNET, *PRIDE AND PREJUDICE*, 1813

'Our pleasures in this world are always to be paid for.'

HENRY TILNEY, *NORTHANGER ABBEY*, 1818

A fondness for reading, which properly directed, must be an education in itself.

MANSFIELD PARK, 1814

'Where so many hours have been spent in convincing myself that
I am right, is there not some reason to fear I may be wrong?'

COLONEL BRANDON, *SENSE AND SENSIBILITY*, 1811

'My idea of good company, Mr Elliot, is the company of clever, well-informed people, who have a great deal of conversation; that is what I call good company.'

ANNE ELLIOT, *PERSUASION*, 1818

Emma denied none of it aloud, and agreed to none of it in private.

EMMA, 1816

'Indulge your imagination in every possible flight.'

ELIZABETH BENNET, PRIDE AND PREJUDICE, 1813

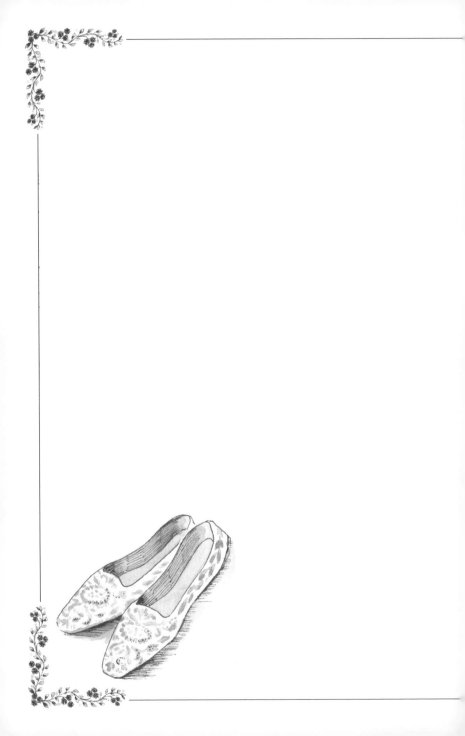

To be fond of dancing was a certain step towards falling in love.

PRIDE AND PREJUDICE, 1813

'Let us have the luxury of silence.'

EDMUND BERTRAM, *MANSFIELD PARK*, 1814

There are people, who the more you do for them,
the less they will do for themselves.

EMMA, 1816

'There is no charm equal to tenderness of heart.'

EMMA, *EMMA*, 1816

By-the-bye, I must leave off being young, I find many douceurs in being a sort of chaperon, for I am put on the sofa near the fire, and can drink as much wine as I like.

LETTER TO CASSANDRA, 6 NOVEMBER 1813

Friendship is certainly the finest balm for the pangs of disappointed love.

NORTHANGER ABBEY, 1818

'There is nothing like staying at home for real comfort.'

MRS ELTON, *EMMA*, 1816

First published in Great Britain in 2015 by Michael O'Mara Books Limited
9 Lion Yard
Tremadoc Road
London SW4 7NQ

A CIP catalogue record for this book is available from the British Library.

Papers used by Michael O'Mara Books Limited are natural, recyclable
products made from wood grown in sustainable forests. The manufacturing
processes conform to the environmental regulations of the country of origin.

ISBN: 978-1-78243-454-2 in print format

2 3 4 5 6 7 8 9 10

www.mombooks.com

Designed and typeset by Ana Bjezancevic
Illustrated by Katie May Green

Printed and bound in China